Everyday Food

pasta

Joyce Bentley

Chrysalis Children's Books

First published in the UK in 2005 by
Chrysalis Children's Books
An imprint of Chrysalis Books Group Plc
The Chrysalis Building, Bramley Road, London W10 6SP

ISBN 1 84458 182 9

British Library Cataloguing in Publication Data
for this book is available from the British Library.

Senior editor *Rasha Elsaeed*
Project editor *Debbie Foy*
Editorial assistant *Camilla Lloyd*
Food consultant *Brenda Alden*
Art director *Sarah Goodwin*
Illustrator *Molly Sage*
Designer *Ben Ruocco, Tall Tree Ltd*
Picture researchers *Sarah Stewart-Richardson, Veneta Bullen, Miguel Lamas*

Printed in China

10 9 8 7 6 5 4 3 2 1

Typography *Natascha Frensch*
Read Regular, READ SMALLCAPS and Read Space; European Community Design Registration 2003
and Copyright © Natascha Frensch 2001-2004 **Read Medium**, **Read Black** and *Read Slanted*
Copyright © Natascha Frensch 2003-2004

READ™ is a revolutionary new typeface that will enhance children's understanding through clear, easily
recognisable character shapes. With its evenly spaced and carefully designed characters, READ™ will help
children at all stages to improve their literacy skills, and is ideal for young readers, reluctant readers and
especially children with dyslexia.

Words in **bold** can be found in Words to remember on page 30.

Picture Acknowledgements
All reasonable efforts have been made to ensure the reproduction of content has been done with the consent of
copyright owners. If you are aware of any unintentional omissions please contact the publishers directly so that
any necessary corrections may be made for future editions.

Anthony Blake Photo Library: Gerrit Buntrock 5, 14, John Sims 19B, Martin Brigdale 21, Eaglemoss Consumer
Publications 23T, Andrew Sydenham 23B; Image courtesy of The Advertising Archives: 7B; akg-images: Tony
Vaccaro 7T; Alamy Images: Gary Cook 19T; Alinari Archives, Florence: 6; Chrysalis Image Library: 10B, 12, Ray
Moller 24T, 24B, 25; Corbis: Owen Franken BC, 13T, Bohemian Nomad Picture 13B, 16, Vittoriano Rastelli
15T, 17, Baumgartner Olivia/SYGM 15B, Michael S. Yamashita 20, Julia Waterlow/Eye Ubiquitous 26; Cephas:
StockFood 10T; Empics: John Walton 27B; Frank Lane Picture Agency: Didier PRIX/Sunset 8, P Breson 9T,
Roger Wilmshurst 4; Pasta Reale Ltd: 18; PowerStock: Stuart Pearce 27T; Rex: Woman's Weekly 22; Royalty
Free: ©Stockbyte FC, 1, 9B, 11

Contents

What is pasta?

Pasta is a type of food. Basic pasta is made from **durum wheat** flour and water. Sometimes egg or oil is added.

The **grains** of durum wheat are at the top of the plant. These are separated from the rest of the plant during **harvesting**.

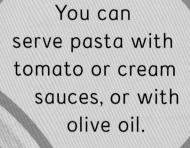

You can serve pasta with tomato or cream sauces, or with olive oil.

We usually eat pasta with sauces or fillings. These sauces can be made with vegetables, fish or meat.

Across the world there are over 600 different pasta shapes to choose from!

Back in time

It is thought that pasta was first discovered in China as far back as 3000 BC. As **explorers** travelled the world it was brought over to Italy and the rest of Europe.

These **medieval** women are preparing and drying pasta.

In Italy pasta used to be dried on racks in the sun.

In 1789, Thomas Jefferson, who became President of the United States, brought the first pasta machine to America. Pasta soon became popular.

This 1960s advert shows a boy enjoying a bowl of spaghetti.

All sorts of pasta

When pasta is made it is cut into shapes. There are many different shapes and sizes. These have Italian names such as ravioli, spaghetti and cannelloni.

Tagliatelle is long, thin ribbons of pasta.

Fusilli means 'little springs'.

Spaghetti means 'little strings'.

These tiny pasta letters are often used in soups.

Macaroni is tube shapes of different lengths.

Farfalle means 'butterflies'.

Making pasta

Pasta flour is made from the inner part of the wheat grain. It is **ground** into a type of flour called **semolina**, then mixed with eggs and water to make a **dough**.

The dough ingredients are measured and often mixed on the table top.

The dough is **kneaded** by rolling and pressing it against a flat surface.

Pasta dough can also have tomato, **beetroot**, spinach and other foods added to give it flavour and colour.

Tricolore is a traditional pasta made with egg, tomato and spinach. It is named after the red, white and green of the Italian flag.

Shaping and drying pasta

The pasta dough is pushed through a machine with holes in it to give the pasta its shape.

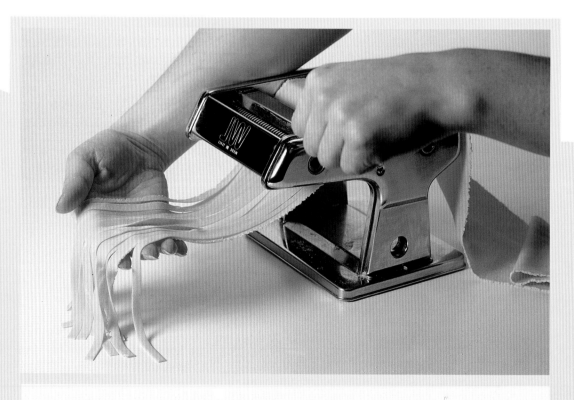

Domestic pasta machines have attachments that can be used to make different pasta shapes.

The shape and size of the holes creates the various pasta shapes. The pasta is allowed to dry for up to two days, until it is **brittle** and ready for cooking or packing.

Cut squares of pasta are filled to make ravioli.

Noodles are made in factories. They are hung over racks to dry.

Cooking pasta

Pasta must be cooked before it is eaten. **Dried pasta** is cooked in boiling water until it is slightly soft. This is called **al dente**.

Dried pasta takes about 12 minutes to cook.

Fresh pasta cooks quickly in a few minutes. To make ravioli, the filling is cooked before being **sealed** into the pasta shapes.

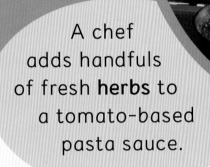

A chef adds handfuls of fresh **herbs** to a tomato-based pasta sauce.

Fresh pasta is not allowed to dry. It is **sprinkled** with flour to stop it from sticking.

15

In the factory

Pasta is made in large quantities in a factory. The dough is made in containers called **vats**. Machines then shape the pasta.

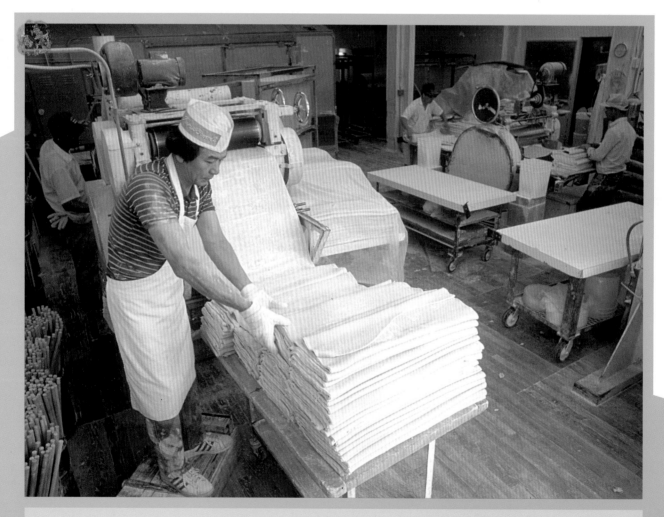

Pasta dough is made into large, flat sheets before it is put through special machines that cut it into shape.

Lengths of pasta are cut using sharp blades. It is dried by large driers that blow hot air at the pasta as it goes along the **conveyor belt**.

Pasta is packed into **airtight** packages to keep it fresh.

Getting to you

In the factory the pasta is weighed and packed by machines before being loaded into crates. The information on the packet tells us how to cook the pasta, what it weighs and how to store it.

Lorries travel across the country to deliver pasta to shops.

Italian dried pasta comes in a variety of shapes and colours.

You can buy pasta in packets in the supermarket. A special shop called a **delicatessen** sells fresh pasta as well as **imported** Italian dried pasta.

Fresh pasta is often made in delicatessens and sold the same day.

Eating pasta

There are many ways to serve pasta. Most pasta is eaten with a tomato, cream or herb sauce. You can add cheese, vegetables, meat or fish to pasta dishes.

Lasagne is made with pasta sheets and layers of minced meat, tomatoes and cream sauce.

Pasta can also be put into salads, bakes and soups. In Italy, it is eaten with just a little sauce to cover it.

The Italians name their pasta after its shape. For example, vermicelli means 'little worms' and conchiglie means 'shells'.

Pesto sauce is a very popular sauce for pasta. It is made from olive oil, basil and **pine nuts**.

Everyone loves pasta

Pasta is enjoyed around the world. It forms part of a **staple diet** for many people as it is cheap and readily available.

This Japanese dish is called ramen. It is a soup made with egg noodles, meat or fish and vegetables.

The Chinese eat lots of noodles. These have been fried to make them crispy.

Many countries have their own special pasta recipes made with locally grown **produce**.

Linguini is thin ribbons of pasta. Here it is cooked with chicken, pesto sauce and **Parmesan** cheese.

A balanced diet

Pasta is a **carbohydrate**, which comes from the wheat grain used to make the flour. Pasta made with egg contains **protein** and **wholemeal** pasta is a good source of **fibre**.

Other carbohydrates include potatoes, bread and rice.

Fruit and vegetables contain carbohydrates and provide lots of **vitamins** and fibre.

For a balanced diet, most of the food we eat should come from the groups at the bottom of the chart and less from the top.

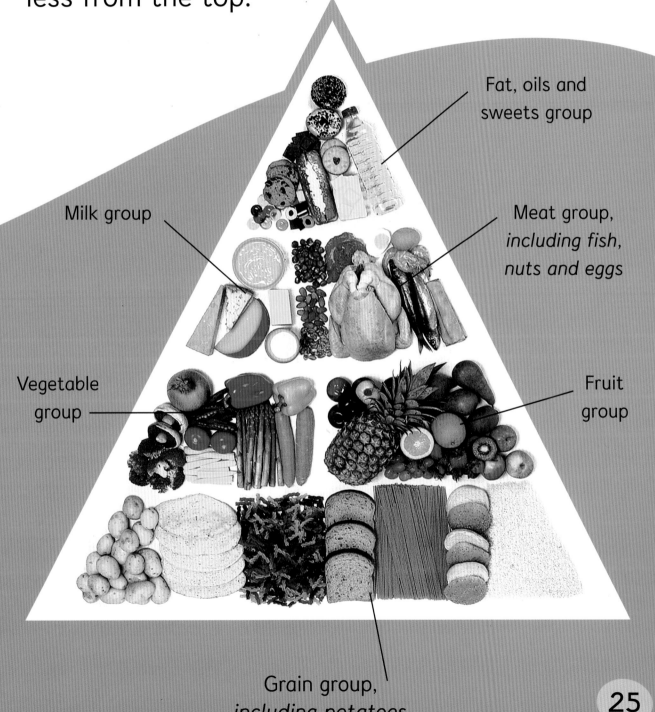

Fat, oils and sweets group

Milk group

Meat group, *including fish, nuts and eggs*

Vegetable group

Fruit group

Grain group, *including potatoes*

Healthy pasta

The carbohydrates in pasta give us energy. People who lead active lives need more carbohydrates than those who are less active.

The protein in egg noodles helps us to grow and stay healthy.

Children use up lots of energy when they are playing, so they need plenty of carbohydrates.

Pasta is good for athletes as it releases energy over a long period of time.

Pasta salad

This colourful dish tastes great on its own or eaten with garlic bread. Serves 2

Children in the kitchen must be supervised at all times by an adult.

YOU WILL NEED

- 100g/4 oz cooked, cooled pasta shapes
- 4 cherry tomatoes
- 2-cm/1-in piece cucumber
- 75g/3 oz cheese
- Olive oil
- Black pepper

1. Chop the cucumber
and cheese into cubes.

2. Cut the tomatoes in half.

3. Mix the pasta and other
ingredients together in a bowl
and pour over a little olive oil.

4. Add some black
pepper and serve!

Words to remember

airtight No air can get in or out.

al dente Cooked until firm to the bite.

beetroot Round, purple root vegetable.

brittle Hard but breaks easily.

carbohydrate A nutrient the body needs for energy.

conveyor belt Machine that carries things along.

delicatessen Shop that sells meats, cheeses and imported foods.

domestic Things that are made for the home.

dough A flour, water (and sometimes egg) mixture.

dried pasta Pasta that has been allowed to dry thoroughly.

durum wheat A kind of plant. The wheat grains are crushed to make flour.

explorers People who travel in search of new places.

fibre Material found in some foods that helps digestion.

fresh pasta Pasta that has not been allowed to dry.

grain The seeds at the top of a cereal plant.

ground To crush something into a powder.

harvesting Pulling crops from the ground when they are ready to eat.

herbs Plants that are used to flavour food.

imported To bring food in from another country to sell.

kneaded To squeeze and press dough to soften it.

medieval A time in history between the 5th and 15th centuries.

Parmesan Hard, dry cheese often sprinkled on top of pasta.

pine nuts The edible seeds of some pine trees.

protein A nutrient that is necessary for growth and repair.

produce Food that is made to sell.

sealed To fasten something so that nothing gets in or out.

semolina Flour that is made from grinding durum wheat grains.

sprinkled To scatter over something.

staple diet Food that forms the main part of the diet.

tricolore The flag of Italy that is red, green and white.

vats Large containers used in factories.

vitamins Nutrients we need for health and to prevent illness.

wholemeal Pasta made from flour that uses the whole grain.

Index